THE
5 LOVE LANGUAGES®
· FOR MEN ·
WORKBOOK

THE
5 LOVE
LANGUAGES®

· FOR MEN ·

#1 *NEW YORK TIMES* BESTSELLER
Gary Chapman

WORKBOOK

NORTHFIELD PUBLISHING
CHICAGO

© 2023 by
GARY CHAPMAN

Developed with the assistance of Peachtree Publishing Services (www.peachtreeeditorial.com). Special thanks to Randy Southern.
Interior design: Erik M. Peterson
Cover design by Faceout Studio
Cover image of bokeh copyright © 2023 by Ole moda/Shutterstock (1469341238). All rights reserved.

ISBN: 978-0-8024-3300-8

We hope you enjoy this book from Northfield Publishing. Our goal is to provide high-quality, thought-provoking books and products that connect truth to your real needs and challenges. For more information on other books and products that will help you with all your important relationships, go to northfieldpublishing.com or write to:

Northfield Publishing
820 N. LaSalle Boulevard
Chicago, IL 60610

1 3 5 7 9 10 8 6 4 2

Printed in the United States of America

CONTENTS

INTRODUCTION

WELCOME to a labor of love.

The ten lessons in this book were created for one purpose: to strengthen and deepen your loving relationship with your wife. The process won't be easy. Nothing worthwhile ever is. This study will pose some challenging questions. It will take you outside your comfort zone. It will even require you to do homework.

But this isn't busywork. These lessons give you workable strategies for applying the principles of *The 5 Love Languages for Men*. They offer glimpses of your relationship's potential when you and your wife speak each other's love language.

If you're working through this study alone, take heart. Your solo efforts will likely have a profound impact on your relationship. Throughout *The 5 Love Languages for Men*, you'll find accounts of extremely dysfunctional relationships that not only survived but thrived thanks to one partner's commitment to learning his or her spouse's love language.

As you work through this study, let patience, grace, and humor be your companions. Learning a new love language can be difficult, and there's more than a little trial and error involved. Show your appreciation for your spouse's efforts to communicate love in ways that are meaningful to you, no matter how clumsy those efforts are at first. And be sure to let him or her know when those efforts hit the mark.

If you're working through this study in a group, pay attention to what your fellow group members share. Inspiration and wisdom can be found in unexpected places. In your interactions with fellow group members, be generous with your encouragement and sparing with your criticism. Ask appropriate follow-up questions to show your interest in other couples' success. See *The 5 Love Languages for Men* Leader's Guide on pages 94–95 for helpful suggestions in facilitating group discussions.

Regardless of how you approach this study, you should be aware that the lessons in this book will require a significant investment of time and effort. There's a lot of important material in these pages. But it's virtually a risk-free investment. You will see dividends. And the more of yourself you pour into this workbook, the greater your dividends will be.

GARY CHAPMAN

OBJECTIVE

In reading this chapter, you will discover how learning your wife's primary love language allows you to work smarter in making her feel loved.

HOW MANY LANGUAGES DO YOU SPEAK?

INSTRUCTIONS: Complete this first lesson after reading chapter 1 ("How Many Languages Do You Speak?" pp. 13–21) of *The 5 Love Languages for Men*.

KEY TERMS

Primary love language: the method of communicating and experiencing emotional love that causes a person to feel truly loved.

Language barrier: a dynamic that arises when spouses do not share the same primary love language, thereby creating a need for them to learn to speak a new love language.

Dialects: nuances within a love language that communicate love in more specific and powerful ways.

Love tank: the emotional reservoir inside everyone that is filled when people speak to us in our primary love language.

OPENING QUESTIONS

1. What is the most extravagant expression of love you've ever given your wife? Why did you choose that specific way of expressing your love? Describe the effort, planning, or financial sacrifice that went into your expression of love.

2. How was your grand gesture of love received? How did your wife react to it? Was it everything you had hoped for? If so, what did you take away from the experience? If not, what would you do differently next time?

THINK ABOUT IT

3. Dr. Chapman begins the chapter by sharing three stories of guys who went to great lengths to show love to their wives. He then says, **"Unless those guys made their plans with their wives' primary love languages in mind, they could have achieved the same results with"**—what? What is your reaction to that realization?

4. Dr. Chapman writes, **"When you express your love for your wife using her *primary* love language, it's like hitting the sweet spot on a baseball bat or golf club. It just *feels right*—and the results are impressive."** Describe a time when you experienced that feeling of speaking your wife's love language in just the right way, whether you meant to or not.

5. In what areas are you and your wife similar? In what areas are you different? How do those similarities and differences shape your relationship, for better or worse?

6. What differences do you see between your wife's love languages or dialects and your love languages or dialects? How do those differences make themselves known in your relationship?

7. According to Dr. Chapman, **"in the first stages of the relationship, when the couple is drunk with infatuation, they may not notice the language barrier. They may be so eager to please each other that they do things that are out of character. . . . Any concerns they may have about their differences get swept away in the tsunami of romance and excitement."** How does that description align with the early days of your relationship? What "out of character" things did you do when you and your wife were falling in love?

8. Of course, what goes up must come down. Or, as Dr. Chapman puts it, **"as the newness of the relationship wears off and the passion levels subside from their honeymoon crests, the two-language couple settles down into a routine. They go back to what they know best."** How long did your "honeymoon crest" last? What routines did you settle into when it ended? What happened to your respective love tanks as a result?

9. What is the biggest challenge you anticipate in learning to speak your wife's primary love language? What is the biggest payoff you anticipate when you finally become fluent in it?

TAKE IT HOME

Most couples don't think about love languages in the early stages of their relationship. The adrenaline and excitement of new love is enough to fill their love tanks. But after the "honeymoon phase" wears off, most couples revert to their natural state and try to communicate using their own primary love languages. Unfortunately, that usually creates a language barrier. No matter how hard the couple tries to show love to each other, unless they learn each other's love language, their attempts will fall flat and their love tanks will slowly empty.

Think about how that cycle has played out—or might play out—in your relationship. For each of the following situations, write what your first instinct would be to show love to your wife. Then come up with a more effective strategy, based on what you know of your wife's actual love language.

	FIRST INSTINCT	BETTER OPTION
It's your anniversary.		
You and your wife just had a major argument.		
Your wife is facing a huge decision or considering a major life change.		
You notice something amazing about your wife—something that makes you love her even more.		
Your wife is feeling insecure about her physical appearance.		

SEVEN KEYS TO SUCCESS

Dr. Chapman identifies seven keys to success in learning your wife's love language. Carefully consider each one as you write your answers to the following questions. Your responses will help you develop a strategy and give you direction as you prepare for the exciting journey ahead.

SHORT MEMORY

What are some past experiences you need to forget or laugh off so that you can move forward in learning to speak your wife's primary love language?

CREATIVITY

What would "thinking outside the box" look like in your life as you attempt to learn your wife's love language?

LISTENING TO GOOD ADVICE

Of all the people you know, whose relationships do you most admire? Explain. Given the opportunity, what questions would you like to ask those couples?

VISION

What adjustments can you make to your daily routine to help you spot new opportunities to show love to your wife?

ENDURANCE

What past accomplishments can you draw on for motivation and inspiration as you press on to master your wife's love language?

PRAYER

If you were to make a prayer list for your relationship—specifically, things you need to be the best husband you can be for your wife—what would be on it? Where can you find time in your daily schedule to take those requests to God?

FIRM STANCE

What adjustments can you make to your schedule, your priorities, or your attitude to show your wife that nothing is more important than your relationship with her?

LOVE CHALLENGE

One of the keys to success in learning your wife's love language is listening to good advice. What steps will you take this week to draw on the wisdom and experience of people whose relationships you admire?

STEP 1

STEP 2

STEP 3

STEP 4

STEP 5

STEP 6

Use this space for more notes, quotes, or lessons learned from the chapter.

OBJECTIVE

In reading this chapter, you will learn how to use words of affirmation
to express love in ways that fill your wife's love tank.

HOW TO BECOME FLUENT IN WORDS OF AFFIRMATION (LOVE LANGUAGE #1)

INSTRUCTIONS: Complete this second lesson after reading chapter 2 ("How to Become Fluent in Words of Affirmation [Love Language #1]," pp. 23–37) of *The 5 Love Languages for Men*.

KEY TERM

Words of affirmation: verbal and written expressions of love, appreciation, and encouragement that communicate love in profound ways for people who speak that love language.

OPENING QUESTIONS

1. King Solomon wrote, "The tongue has the power of life and death" (Proverbs 18:21). When was the last time someone said something that made you feel truly alive? Why do you think those words had such an impact on you?

2. When was the last time you said something for the purpose of making someone else's life a little better? How were your words received?

THINK ABOUT IT

3. Dr. Chapman says, **"The *real* power of words lies in their ability to fill people's love tanks. If your wife's primary love language is words of affirmation, that power is at your fingertips—or, more specifically, at the tip of your tongue. How you feel about wielding that power will depend on your own primary love language."** How *do* you feel about that power? What is your reaction when you consider that the way you use your words can change your wife's life?

4. Dr. Chapman emphasizes that flattery is not a dialect of the words of affirmation love language. Why does flattery often have the opposite effect as words of affirmation? What must be true if your words are going to make a difference in your wife's life?

5. "Love is kind." Those three simple words can and should guide your communication with your wife. But, as Dr. Chapman explains, **"it can be a challenge for a lot of guys. From an early age, we're conditioned to wield words like weapons."** That conditioning shows itself through sarcasm and biting humor. Why are those two types of speech counterproductive to words of affirmation?

6. Words of affirmation can be especially powerful during times of conflict. What does Dr. Chapman say is your best strategy when your wife is angry, upset, and lashing out with provocative words? Instead of trying to prove your own correctness or superiority in that situation, what should be your goal with your words?

7. In talking about people's inability to forgive their spouse, Dr. Chapman writes, **"I am amazed by how many individuals mess up every new day with yesterday."** How have you seen that play out in your own relationship? Give an example of how you could use words of affirmation in expressing not just love but also forgiveness to your wife.

8. **"Love makes requests, not demands."** That's how Dr. Chapman summarizes the importance of humility in speaking words of affirmation. We all have desires that we want our spouse to know about. What happens when we express our desires in the form of demands? In contrast, what happens when we express our desires in the form of requests?

9. Where do you see the biggest opportunities to make a difference in your wife's life by becoming more purposeful in using words of affirmation? What do you envision as the toughest challenges you'll face in incorporating words of affirmation into your daily routine?

TAKE IT HOME

In addition to praising your wife directly, one of the most powerful ways to use words of affirmation is to praise your wife to others, especially her friends and acquaintances. As a result, they may pass that praise back to her! To get in the habit of praising her to others, write down the names of four people and specific compliments you can share with them about your wife.

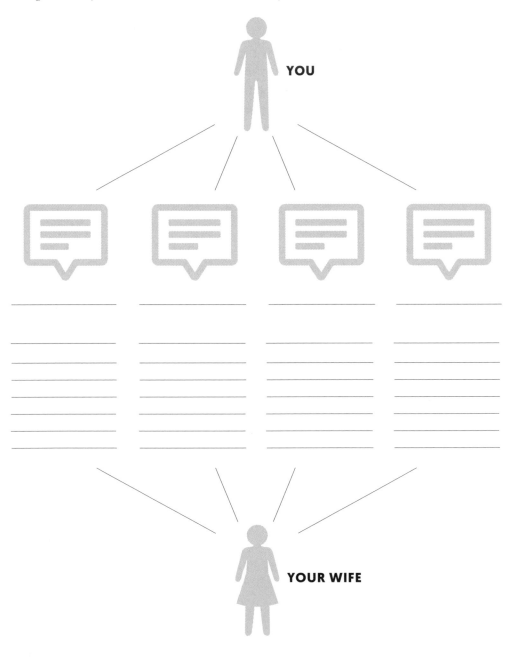

UNTAPPED POTENTIAL

Words of affirmation can give your wife the confidence and encouragement she needs to tap into her potential and step out of her comfort zone to fulfill that potential. For your words to be effective, though, they need to be purposeful and on-target. Here are a few questions that can help you maximize your words' potential.

What is important to your wife?

What is your wife capable of doing if she could tap into her full potential?

What specific words of affirmation can you offer to help her fulfill her potential?

How can you make sure that you don't inadvertently pressure her into doing something you think she should do?

What impact would you like your words of affirmation to have on your wife?

LOVE CHALLENGE

Mark Twain once said, "I can live for two months on a good compliment." But what if the goal wasn't merely to live but to thrive? What are some heartfelt compliments you can give to your wife? Continue to observe things she does on a daily basis and find ways to communicate your love to her for those things.

Use this space for more notes, quotes, or lessons learned from the chapter.

OBJECTIVE

In reading this chapter, you will learn how to use quality time, quality conversation, and quality activities to express love in ways that fill your wife's love tank.

HOW TO BECOME FLUENT IN QUALITY TIME (LOVE LANGUAGE #2)

INSTRUCTIONS: Complete this third lesson after reading chapter 3 ("How to Become Fluent in Quality Time [Love Language #2]," pp. 39–53) of *The 5 Love Languages for Men*.

KEY TERMS

Quality time: a way of expressing love through spending purposeful time with, and directing your full attention to, another person.

Quality conversation: empathetic dialogue in which two people share their experiences, thoughts, feelings, and desires in a friendly, uninterrupted context.

OPENING QUESTIONS

1. On a scale of one to ten, with one being "time is an abstract concept; it has no meaning to me" and ten being "time is our most precious commodity," how valuable is your time to you? Where did your attitude toward time come from?

2. If you had an extra two hours every day, what would you do with them? How would your life be different with two extra hours per day?

THINK ABOUT IT

3. If your wife's primary love language is quality time, Dr. Chapman explains how your wife feels loved and genuinely cared for when you go "the extra mile" by spending focused time with her. What does going the extra mile look like when spending time with your wife?

4. Dr. Chapman emphasizes that there's a huge difference between spending time with your wife and spending quality time with her. Give an example from your own relationship of the difference between spending time together and spending quality time together. According to Dr. Chapman, what is the key to establishing the right mindset for quality time?

5. One of the most common dialects of the quality time love language is quality conversation. According to Dr. Chapman, what are the three things you communicate to your spouse when you engage in quality conversation? What is a surefire way of drawing your wife into quality conversation? What does empathetic listening look like in your relationship? What are some questions that would show your real desire to understand your wife?

6. After telling the story of Patrick, the regretful man who realized too late what his wife really needed from him, Dr. Chapman asks, **"Anyone care to cast the first stone here?"** Why is it so tempting to try to solve a problem or offer advice when your wife talks about certain struggles she's dealing with? How does that problem-solving instinct get in the way of quality conversation?

7. Dr. Chapman writes, **"Most of us have little training in listening. We're far more proficient in thinking and speaking. That lack of training will be hard to hide if your wife's primary love language is quality time and her dialect is quality conversation."** What are the five practical tips he offers for acquiring the skill of listening? Which one would present the biggest challenge for you? Why?

8. According to Dr. Chapman, **"self-revelation is a challenge for many guys."** What childhood experiences can make self-revelation difficult later in life? What is the biggest challenge you face in becoming more emotionally revealing to your wife? What specific steps can you take to overcome that challenge?

9. Quality activities is also a dialect of the quality time love language. Dr. Chapman emphasizes, **"Quality activities may include anything in which one or both of you have an interest. The emphasis is not on what you're doing but on *why* you're doing it. The purpose is to experience something together, to have your wife walk away from it, thinking, *He cares about me. He was willing to do something with me that I enjoy, and he did it with a positive attitude.*"** With that in mind, what are some quality activities that would fill your wife's love tank? How can you make those activities especially memorable for her?

TAKE IT HOME

Where does the time go? It's a question everyone would do well to answer. But for the husband of someone whose primary love language is quality time, understanding how you use the twenty-four hours allotted to you every day is absolutely essential.

The pie chart below represents a typical day—twenty-four hours' worth of time. Your assignment is to fill in, as accurately as possible, how you allot that time, using categories such as sleep, work (including commute), eating, exercise, screen time (including social media, TV, online browsing, and video games), hobbies and pastimes, chores, family obligations (such as soccer games or dance recitals), church, community service, and, of course, alone time with your wife.

Your goal here is to reflect an average day as it is, not as you would like it to be. Be as accurate as possible in your allotment of time.

WHERE *CAN* THE TIME GO?

The pie chart below reflects a *potential* day—an allotment of twenty-four hours designed to maximize your quality time with your wife. In what areas can you cut back to devote more time to her? Let this pie chart reflect your cuts and your new priorities.

In the space below, write some specific ideas for adjusting your daily schedule to open up more time to spend with your wife. In some cases, it might mean cutting back in some areas—say, screen time—and using the time saved to devote to your wife, perhaps in the form of an evening walk. In other cases, it might mean finding ways to include your wife in certain activities. For example, you might start exercising or cooking meals together. With a little creativity and sacrifice, you can find a surprising number of ways to spend more quality time with your wife.

LOVE CHALLENGE

If tomorrow follows the pattern of every other day since the day of your birth, you will have twenty-four hours to spend. What special gesture can you make in the next twenty-four hours to signal to your wife that you want to prioritize quality time with her?

Use this space for more notes, quotes, or lessons learned from the chapter.

OBJECTIVE

In reading this chapter, you will learn how to use well-chosen gifts
to express love in ways that fill your wife's love tank.

HOW TO BECOME FLUENT IN GIFT GIVING (LOVE LANGUAGE #3)

INSTRUCTIONS: Complete this fourth lesson after reading chapter 4 ("How to Become Fluent in Gift Giving [Love Language #3]," pp. 55–67) of *The 5 Love Languages for Men.*

KEY TERM

Gift giving: a love language in which a person experiences emotional wholeness through well-chosen presents.

OPENING QUESTIONS

1. If you could give your wife one gift, what would it be? Let your imagination run wild. Don't limit your thinking to things that are realistically possible for you. For example, if your wife still talks about the trip the two of you took to Italy, your gift might be a stunning lakeside villa you both admired there. If your wife is still grieving the loss of her father, your gift might be one more day to spend with him in perfect health.

2. What is the closest approximation of that gift that you could realistically give your wife? For example, you obviously couldn't give her a day with her late father, but you could create a video compilation of scenes of your wife and her father together.

THINK ABOUT IT

3. In Dr. Chapman's story of Erik and Kelsey, Erik's gift of a baseball was still precious to Kelsey fifteen years later. What are some likely reasons that specific gift held such special meaning for her? What did Erik likely learn about Kelsey based on her reaction to the very first gift he gave her? How might he have built on what he learned going forward in their relationship?

4. As you look around your house, what souvenirs, mementos, or photos do you see that reflect your wife's gift giving love language? What special meaning is attached to each one?

5. Dr. Chapman writes, **"Of the five love languages, gift giving is the one most likely to raise an eyebrow or two."** Why is it so likely to raise some questions? What's the first step in avoiding the appearance of materialism or gold digging in speaking the love language?

6. According to Dr. Chapman, what drives a husband to learn his wife's gift giving love language? What is the wife's aim in placing such a high priority on gifts? (Hint: It's not materialism.)

7. Describe some of your earliest experiences with the connection between love and gifts. How much of those early instincts are still with you? For people whose primary love language is gift giving, what is even more delightful and meaningful than the gift itself?

8. According to Dr. Chapman, **"if your wife's primary love language is gift giving, the cost of the gift will matter to her only if it's greatly out of line with what you can afford—or what you spend on yourself or others."** If you spend too much and put yourself in a financial hole, everyone suffers. If you don't spend enough, you'll look cheap and selfish, and your gift may insult your wife instead of making her feel loved. With those parameters in mind, what types of gifts would be ideal for your wife?

9. In the "Storytellers" sidebar, Dr. Chapman points out that **"an effective story-gift combo is one that gives your wife some insight into the way your mind works when it's thinking about her."** What story-gift combo would give your wife a glimpse into your gift-giving process?

TAKE IT HOME

When it comes to gifts, one size does *not* fit all. One person's meaningful present is another person's useless trinket. One person's thoughtful gesture is another person's wasted opportunity. To get a sense of your wife's preferences, circle the item in each of the following pairs that you think she would appreciate more—the one that you think would speak love to her more clearly.

Giving her a gift card to her favorite store
and taking her on a mini shopping spree

OR

Choosing an item from that store that you
think she would like, without consulting her

A spa day

OR

An overnight hotel stay

Jewelry

OR

Clothing

The gift of a day, involving just the two of you, where she
gets to choose the places you go and the things you do

OR

The gift of a day to herself, while you take care
of the kids and/or household responsibilities

A greeting card with your heartfelt
sentiments written in it

OR

A framed selfie of the two of you

Donating to a nonprofit organization
your wife supports

OR

Buying stock in a company
whose products she swears by

Hiding a small, inexpensive (and TSA-friendly)
gift in her luggage when she leaves for a trip

OR

Preparing a series of elaborate clues that lead to
a relatively expensive (the kind you can afford no
more than once a year), beautifully wrapped present

Dinner at her favorite restaurant
and a movie in a theater

OR

Takeout from her favorite restaurant
and a movie at home

A flower from a street vendor

OR

A pint of ice cream

A star registered in your wife's name

OR

An item she collects

As you look over your responses, how would you summarize your wife's preferences? To put it another way, what specific dialects does your wife prefer in the love language of receiving gifts? Does she prefer homemade or store-bought gifts? Does she prefer to receive frequent, inexpensive presents or infrequent, expensive ones? Does she prefer practical items or whimsical novelties?

SEVEN DAYS OF GIVING

On the calendar below, plan a special week of gift giving. Think of something special you can give your wife each day. You don't have to ruin your budget. Remember, gifts don't have to be expensive to be meaningful. But all seven should be meaningful. You might also write down some creative ideas as to where and how you might give each gift.

SUNDAY	
MONDAY	
TUESDAY	
WEDNESDAY	
THURSDAY	
FRIDAY	
SATURDAY	

LOVE CHALLENGE

In questions 1 and 2 of this lesson, you imagined the ideal gift for your wife and the closest approximation to that ideal gift that you could think of. What steps will you take this week to make that approximation happen and prepare to give a memorable gift to your wife?

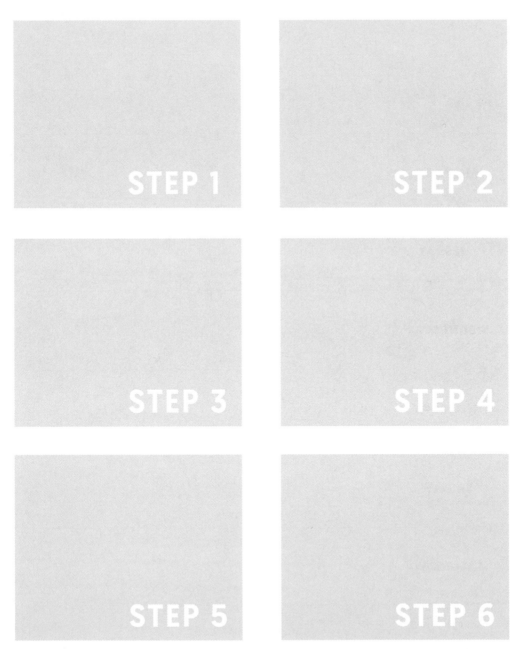

STEP 1

STEP 2

STEP 3

STEP 4

STEP 5

STEP 6

Use this space for more notes, quotes, or lessons learned from the chapter.

OBJECTIVE

In reading this chapter, you will learn how to perform tasks
and complete projects in ways that fill your wife's love tank.

HOW TO BECOME FLUENT IN ACTS OF SERVICE (LOVE LANGUAGE #4)

INSTRUCTIONS: Complete this fifth lesson after reading chapter 5 ("How to Become Fluent in Acts of Service [Love Language #4]," pp. 69–81) of *The 5 Love Languages for Men.*

KEY TERM

Acts of service: a love language in which a person experiences emotional wholeness when chores or tasks are done for his or her benefit.

OPENING QUESTIONS

1. Have you or anyone you know ever worked in the service industry? If so, what was the experience like? What was your takeaway from the experience? What did you learn about people—and yourself—from providing tangible services?

2. How are chores and household responsibilities assigned in your home? Are there certain chores no one likes doing? If so, which ones? Are there certain chores your wife specifically dislikes? If so, which ones? Why?

THINK ABOUT IT

3. In the story Dr. Chapman used at the beginning of the chapter, Andre imagined how his rugby teammates and his father would react to seeing him clean the bathroom. Who shaped your ideas about what a man should or shouldn't do around the house? How do those ideas reinforce or get in the way of your efforts to learn the love language of acts of service?

4. How would you summarize the "bad news" and "good news" Dr. Chapman offers concerning the importance of impact? Ultimately, when it comes to acts of service, what is the only criterion for judgment? What two questions should guide your actions?

5. Dr. Chapman suggests inviting your wife to compile her "dream to-do list"—the acts of service that would make her feel most loved. What is critical for you to do as soon as you receive her list? Why is initiative so much more important than good intentions? What would be your preferred strategy for showing initiative when it comes to your wife's list?

6. According to Dr. Chapman, **"the key to initiating acts of service is to make it a '3-D experience' with Drive, Discipline, and Dedication."** What does "Drive" refer to? How can you remind yourself of why you're working to become fluent in acts of service? What does "Discipline" refer to? What sacrifices may be necessary for you to show love to your wife through some especially ambitious acts of service? What does "Dedication" refer to? What happens when dedication fades?

7. Dr. Chapman writes, **"The right thing done with the wrong attitude can actually cause more harm than good."** Why? What three ingredients are essential for your acts of service to have maximum impact? Give examples of how you could demonstrate each of them while performing an act of service for your wife.

8. **"Of the five love languages, acts of service seems to have the most potential for abuse. . . . Manipulation by guilt ('If you were a good wife, you would do this for me') is not the language of love. Coercion by fear ('You will do this or you will be sorry') is alien to love."** After identifying the potential problem, Dr. Chapman reveals the strategy for addressing it. How do you remove fear, guilt, and resentment from the acts of service love language?

9. How can you prepare yourself for the inevitable trial and error that will occur as you work to become fluent in acts of service? How can you embrace your wife's constructive criticism without allowing it to derail your motivation?

TAKE IT HOME

Rank the following ideas for becoming fluent in acts of service from one to six, according to how feasible they are for you (one would be the easiest for you to put into practice; six would be the most difficult). Next to each one, write some ideas as to how you could make it work.

_____ Plan to get up a half hour earlier or stay up a half hour later every day to work on an act of service for your wife.

_____ Make dinner—and clean the kitchen afterward—at least two nights a week.

_____ Plan a weekly act of service you and your wife can work on together. For example, the two of you might volunteer at a homeless shelter or a rescue animal shelter.

_____ Run interference for your wife so that she can have some alone time two or three evenings a week. That may involve keeping your kids occupied, making lunches for the next day, or finishing household chores.

_____ Trade services with another husband. If you think of an act of service that's beyond your skill set, bring in assistance. In return, offer your own specialized skills and expertise for something your "subcontractor" needs to get done.

_____ Build a network of advisers—made up of people who know your wife and perhaps even other husbands who are trying to learn the acts of service love language—to assist you in your efforts to become fluent in your wife's love language.

HOW MUCH WOULD IT MEAN? (TWO PERSPECTIVES)

Below you'll find a list of acts of service. Rate each one on a scale of one to ten, based on how meaningful you think it would be to your wife, with one being "not meaningful at all" and ten being "extremely meaningful." We've left two slots blank for you to fill in with ideas that are specific to your relationship. After you've rated all of them, ask your wife to do the same. Compare your numbers and talk about areas where there are notable discrepancies.

ACT OF SERVICE	YOU	WIFE
Washing and vacuuming her car once a month		
Making dinner twice a week		
Vacuuming your floors		
Doing laundry		
Washing, drying, and putting away dishes		
Mowing and edging the lawn, trimming the bushes		
Cleaning out your garage		
Shopping for groceries		
Dealing with paperwork		
Repairing a broken item in your house		
Taking on childcare responsibilities		

LOVE CHALLENGE

Is there a chore that you've been meaning to do forever but never seem to have the time (or energy or motivation) to tackle? One that gets grandfathered onto every household to-do list but never gets crossed off? Something your wife has likely given up hope of ever seeing completed? Finishing that task would be a great way of announcing your intention to learn her love language. What steps do you need to take this week to complete that task and cross it off your to-do list?

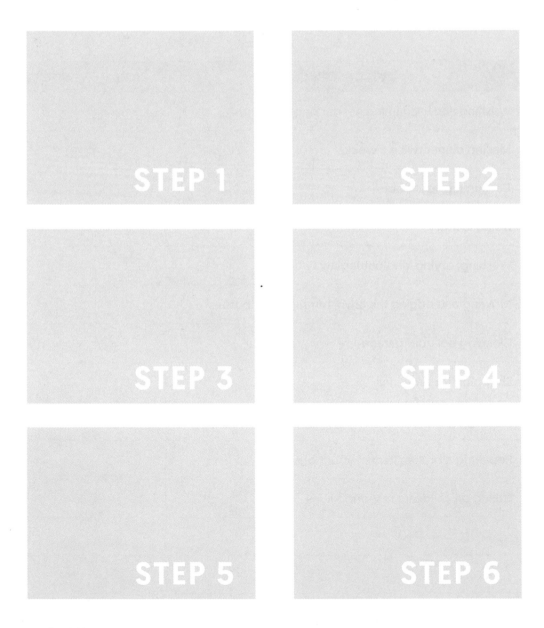

STEP 1

STEP 2

STEP 3

STEP 4

STEP 5

STEP 6

Use this space for more notes, quotes, or lessons learned from the chapter.

OBJECTIVE

In reading this chapter, you will learn how to use
physical touch in ways that fill your wife's love tank.

HOW TO BECOME FLUENT IN PHYSICAL TOUCH (LOVE LANGUAGE #5)

INSTRUCTIONS: Complete this sixth lesson after reading chapter 6 ("How to Become Fluent in Physical Touch [Love Language #5]," pp. 83–95) of *The 5 Love Languages for Men.*

KEY TERM

Physical touch: a love language in which a person experiences emotional wholeness through human contact.

OPENING QUESTIONS

1. List three types of touch that drive you crazy—in a good way. Why do those types of touch have such an impact on you? List three types of touch that drive you crazy—in a not-so-good way. Why do they irritate you?

2. From your own experience or the experiences of people you know, list three reasons why a guy may not be naturally "touchy-feely." How do you react when you're put in a position of having to make physical contact with someone you don't know well? Do you think people get the wrong idea about you based on your attitude toward physical contact? Explain.

THINK ABOUT IT

3. What role does physical contact play in your daily life—not just with your wife and family but with work associates, friends, teammates, and new acquaintances? Do you generally initiate handshakes, hugs, high fives, pats on the back—or do you wait for others to initiate?

4. Dr. Chapman writes, **"After the honeymoon period, when the newlyweds can't get enough of each other, many couples settle into a pattern of ever-increasing physical distance."** How would you describe the physical touch pattern you and your wife settled into after your "honeymoon period"? How do you explain it? How do you feel about it?

5. According to Dr. Chapman, if your wife's primary love language is physical touch, **"physical contact that wouldn't even register with most people has the potential to thrill her, change her mood, brighten her day, and—most importantly—make her feel loved and cared for."** What evidence do you see of that potential in your wife? How does she make her need for physical contact known?

6. Dr. Chapman recommends doing a "baseline test," using the same principle that high school sports programs use for their concussion protocols, to measure your current physical touch relationship with your wife. What do you think your baseline physical touch test would show? How many times would you estimate that you touch your wife during an average day? How do you feel about it? How do you think your wife feels about it? Where do you see room for improvement?

7. Dr. Chapman offers a valuable reminder: **"In reality, not all touches are created equal. Some will bring more pleasure to her than others."** With that in mind, who is your best instructor? What are the only touches available to you? What happens if you insist on touching her in *your* way and in *your* time?

8. **"Surely a red-blooded, testosterone-driven man can be forgiven for smiling slyly when he discovers that his wife experiences love primarily through physical touch. . . . After all, physical touch *does* include sex, right?"** How does Dr. Chapman answer that question? What important reminder does he offer about the purpose of becoming fluent in the love language of physical touch? What three points do you need to remember?

9. Think of the last crisis you and your wife faced. How did you react physically to it? Did you use physical touch to comfort and console, or did you withdraw from physical contact? How do you explain your reaction? What do you wish you'd done in that situation? How will you apply the lessons of that experience the next time you face a crisis?

TAKE IT HOME

On the outline below, draw arrows to various body parts and write ideas for using that body part to speak the love language of physical touch to your wife. Some ideas are obvious: holding her hand, kissing her lips, massaging her shoulders. See how many less-than-obvious ideas you can come up with, involving body parts that are often overlooked. For example, brushing your wife's hair or clasping her elbow as you walk into church may fill her love tank more quickly than you expect.

THE RIGHT TOUCH

For each of the following situations, think of a physical touch that would be appropriate, something that would communicate love in an unmistakable way to your wife.

SITUATION	THE RIGHT TOUCH
You walk in the door after work.	
The two of you are cheering for your favorite team.	
The two of you have the house to yourselves for the night.	
The two of you are making up after a heated argument.	
Your wife isn't feeling well.	

LOVE CHALLENGE

According to Dr. Chapman, if you want to become fluent in the love language of physical touch, **"your wife needs to know that your aim is true, your intentions are noble, and your efforts are directed at her."** How will you start that conversation this week? How will you enlist your wife's help and guidance in learning her love language?

Use this space for more notes, quotes, or lessons learned from the chapter.

OBJECTIVE

In reading this chapter, you will learn how to examine
your personal preferences and interactions with your wife
to discover your primary love language.

WHAT LANGUAGES DO YOU SPEAK?

INSTRUCTIONS: Complete this seventh lesson after reading chapter 7 ("What Languages Do You Speak?" pp. 97–107) of *The 5 Love Languages for Men*.

KEY TERM

Negative use of love languages: love language elements that are used in hurtful, damaging ways—or that are simply absent in a relationship—that underscore the importance of their positive use.

OPENING QUESTIONS

1. What words would your wife use to describe you? If you have kids, what words would they use? Your closest friends? Your coworkers? What about people with whom you don't get along? In your opinion, which words come closest to the truth of who you are? Which ones might give hints as to what your primary love language is?

2. How many languages do you speak? Don't limit your thinking to official languages such English and Spanish. How many types of jargon do you speak and understand? Are you fluent in computer technospeak? The vernacular of your favorite hobby? Medical terminology? In how many unofficial dialects are you at least somewhat fluent?

THINK ABOUT IT

3. Did you have an "Aha!" moment the first time you looked at a list of the five love languages? Did one jump out at you as your primary love language? Explain. Did you recognize your wife's primary love language? Explain. How certain are you of your wife's primary love language? How certain are you of your own primary love language? What doubts or questions, if any, keep you from being 100 percent sure?

4. Why are guys especially susceptible to self-deception when it comes to our primary love language? Why is it important to understand the difference between a biological need and an emotional one?

5. If you can't readily identify your primary love language, it might help to think in terms of what hurts you most deeply when a love language is used negatively. What negative use of a love language comes to mind?

6. Examining how you express love to your wife can reveal clues about your primary love language. But it's not necessarily an absolute indicator. Why is it also important to consider the role that learned behavior plays in your expressions of love?

7. Dr. Chapman writes that **"most people marry someone whose primary love language is different from theirs."** If that's the case with you and your spouse, what's the logical first step in coming to grips with your language barrier? If your primary love language is physical touch and your wife's is quality time, what practical matters need to be sorted out first?

8. After discussing the ways in which both of you are comfortable expressing love—that is, your respective primary love languages—you must move on. Dr. Chapman explains it this way: **"Unfortunately, what's comfortable for each of you won't impact the other."** What must you be willing to do to become fluent in your wife's love language? What would that kind of sacrifice look like in your relationship?

9. According to Dr. Chapman, what should you do **"whenever you feel annoyed or frustrated with your wife's attempts to communicate via your love language"**? What roles do appreciation, gratitude, leeway, and understanding play in helping your wife learn to speak your love language?

TAKE IT HOME

If you're not sure what your primary love language is, give careful thought to the following questions. Your answers may tell you what you need to know.

Which of the following complaints sounds most like something you would say to your wife?

_____ "If you ever gave me a real compliment, I'd probably assume you were talking to someone behind me."

_____ "You seem to have time for everyone but me."

_____ "It's exhausting to be the only person who cares about how clean our house is."

_____ "You took a weeklong trip and didn't bring me back anything?"

_____ "Do you find me repulsive? Is that why you refuse to touch me?"

Which of the following would annoy or hurt you the most if your wife did it?

_____ Criticize you in front of others

_____ Cancel a date with you to go out with her friends

_____ Refuse your request to help you with a chore

_____ Give you a thoughtless gift for your birthday

_____ Go to bed without giving you a hug or kiss

Which of the following do you request most often from your wife?

_____ Compliments and encouragement

_____ Alone time, just the two of you

_____ Thoughtful presents

_____ Help with certain household responsibilities

_____ More hand-holding, caressing, hugging, and kissing

If you had your choice, which love language would you use to express your feelings to your wife?

_____ Words of affirmation

_____ Quality time

_____ Giving gifts

_____ Acts of service

_____ Physical touch

DISCOVERING YOUR WIFE'S LOVE LANGUAGE

If you're not sure what your wife's primary love language is, answer the same questions—this time, from her perspective.

Which of the following complaints sounds most like something your wife would say to you?

_____ "If you ever gave me a real compliment, I'd probably assume you were talking to someone behind me."

_____ "You seem to have time for everyone but me."

_____ "It's exhausting to be the only person who cares about how clean our house is."

_____ "You took a weeklong trip and didn't bring me back anything?"

_____ "Do you find me repulsive? Is that why you refuse to touch me?"

Which of the following would annoy or hurt your wife the most if you did it?

_____ Criticize her in front of others

_____ Cancel a date with her to go out with your friends

_____ Refuse her request to help her with a chore

_____ Give her a thoughtless gift for her birthday

_____ Go to bed without giving her a hug or kiss

Which of the following does your wife request most often from you?

_____ Compliments and encouragement

_____ Alone time, just the two of you

_____ Thoughtful presents

_____ Help with certain household responsibilities

_____ More hand-holding, caressing, hugging, and kissing

If your wife had her choice, which love language would she use to express her feelings to you?

_____ Words of affirmation

_____ Quality time

_____ Giving gifts

_____ Acts of service

_____ Physical touch

LOVE CHALLENGE

Dr. Chapman recommends playing "The Tank Check Game" with your wife three times a week for three weeks. That's a significant commitment, especially if the two of you aren't used to opening up to each other in the way the game calls for. How will you introduce your wife to the game this week in a way that piques her interest but doesn't overwhelm her?

Use this space for more notes, quotes, or lessons learned from the chapter.

OBJECTIVE

In reading this chapter, you will learn how to choose
to love your wife in ways that profoundly impact her
rather than relying on ways that are comfortable for you.

TROUBLESHOOTING

INSTRUCTIONS: Complete this eighth lesson after reading chapter 8 ("Troubleshooting," pp. 109–119) of *The 5 Love Languages for Men*.

KEY TERM

In-love experience: a euphoric emotional obsession in which a person fixates on the positive aspects of a romantic partner—and of the relationship—but loses sight of practical realities.

OPENING QUESTIONS

1. Dr. Chapman begins the chapter with these words: **"In an ideal world, a couple would discover each other's love language on their first date."** What did you discover about your wife on your first date? As you look back on it now, did she give you any clues as to her primary love language? If so, what were they?

2. What did your wife discover about you—for better or worse—on your first date? How did she react to the things she learned? Do you think you gave her any clues as to your primary love language? If so, what were they? Did she seem to pick up on them?

THINK ABOUT IT

3. Dr. Chapman writes, **"The reality for many couples is that they allow their feelings of romance, excitement, and 'in-loveness' to carry them into marriage before they've had a chance to consider each other's love language."** If you and your wife had known each other's love languages—as well as the work it would take to become fluent in them—how might that have affected the early stages of your relationship?

4. Dr. Chapman points out that the busyness and pressures of everyday life leave couples little time or energy to learn a new love language. As a result, they tend to stick to the language they know and hope for the best. What's the problem with that strategy?

5. What two options do couples have when **"the 'in-loveness' that carried them to the altar dissipates, leaving two people who bear little resemblance to the starry-eyed lovebirds in their wedding photos"**?

6. Choosing the second option isn't always easy. What happens over time in a marriage when the "ups" aren't quite as high as the couple expected and the "downs" are considerably lower and longer than they had ever thought possible?

7. Dr. Chapman talks about his counseling sessions with Brent and Becky. What happened during their twelve years of marriage that led them to that place? Do you see any parallels to your own relationship? If so, what insight or advice would you have offered them? If not, why did your relationship take a different turn?

8. What does Dr. Chapman identify as his wife's primary love language? What is one of his key strategies for speaking that love language? Why is that strategy especially challenging for him? Why does that make his efforts even more impactful for his wife?

9. On a scale of one to ten, with ten being the highest, how equipped are you to communicate in your spouse's primary love language? Explain. On a scale of one to ten, how motivated are you to learn your spouse's primary love language? Explain.

TAKE IT HOME

Dr. Chapman wraps up the chapter with a simple yet profound thought: *Love is a choice.* Not a once-and-for-all choice that you make on the day of your wedding, but a continuous series of choices. Every day brings new choices—new opportunities for you and your wife to deepen your love for each other by making tough decisions to work hard for your relationship or to slowly drift apart by making easy decisions to take the path of least resistance.

For each of the following situations, write an easy choice and a hard choice you would face in dealing with that situation. For example, if your parenting style clashes with your wife's parenting style, the easy choice might be for each of you to follow your own instincts and drop subtle criticisms of the other in front of your kids. The hard choice might be to show some humility, work out a compromise, and develop a united parenting style that incorporates your combined strengths and plays to both of your primary love languages.

You and your wife would love to become fluent in each other's love language, but with your work, family, social, and household responsibilities, you don't have the time.

EASY CHOICE	HARD CHOICE

You've been making a genuine effort to become fluent in your wife's love language, but you have little to show for it. Everything you do is met with criticism or indifference.

EASY CHOICE	HARD CHOICE

Your wife shows zero interest in learning to speak your primary love language.

EASY CHOICE	HARD CHOICE

You and your wife have ignored each other's primary love languages since the "honeymoon phase" of your relationship. Your love tanks are empty and have been for as long as you can remember.

EASY CHOICE	HARD CHOICE

IMPLICATIONS

For each of the situations you considered on the previous pages, write down what would happen—good and bad—if you made the easy choice and if you made the hard choice. For example, if you made the hard choice in the first situation and carved out time to learn each other's love language, you might have to sacrifice (temporarily, at least) things that are important to you.

You and your wife would love to become fluent in each other's love language, but with your work, family, social, and household responsibilities, you don't have the time.

IF YOU MAKE THE EASY CHOICE...	IF YOU MAKE THE HARD CHOICE...

You've been making a genuine effort to become fluent in your wife's love language, but you have little to show for it. Everything you do is met with criticism or indifference.

IF YOU MAKE THE EASY CHOICE...	IF YOU MAKE THE HARD CHOICE...

Your wife shows zero interest in learning to speak your primary love language.

IF YOU MAKE THE EASY CHOICE...	IF YOU MAKE THE HARD CHOICE...

You and your wife have ignored each other's primary love languages since the "honeymoon phase" of your relationship. Your love tanks are empty and have been for as long as you can remember.

IF YOU MAKE THE EASY CHOICE...	IF YOU MAKE THE HARD CHOICE...

LOVE CHALLENGE

Strong, healthy, thriving relationships take hard work. If you and your wife have a strong relationship or you are working toward a strong relationship, at various points along the way, you've made hard choices. You've refused to take the path of least resistance. What will you do for your wife this week to celebrate the hard work you've both put into your relationship? What will you say to commit yourself to making wise—and difficult—choices in the future?

Use this space for more notes, quotes, or lessons learned from the chapter.

OBJECTIVE

In reading this chapter, you will learn how to embrace
the reality of anger in your relationship and find a workable
strategy for dealing with it in a healthy way.

HOW CAN YOU WORK THROUGH ANGER TOGETHER?

INSTRUCTIONS: Complete this ninth lesson after reading chapter 9 ("How Can You Work Through Anger Together?" pp. 121–135) of *The 5 Love Languages for Men*.

KEY TERMS

Definitive anger: anger that is sparked by someone else's wrong actions.

Distorted anger: anger that is sparked when your spouse says or does something that irritates you, or they fail to do it "your way."

OPENING QUESTIONS

1. What's the most ridiculous thing you've ever seen someone get angry about? What were the circumstances? How did other people react to the person's anger? How was the situation resolved?

2. If you could take back one angry outburst—one fit of rage—in your past, what would it be? What was it that set you off? How bad did it get? How did the person who bore the brunt of your anger react? What do you wish you'd done differently?

THINK ABOUT IT

3. Dr. Chapman begins the chapter with the story of Dan and Sarah. What did Sarah do that provoked Dan's anger? What did Dan do—or not do—that provoked Sarah's anger? If this were you and your wife speaking frankly about your anger, which details would be different?

4. According to Dr. Chapman, the first step in managing anger in a healthy way is to acknowledge the reality of it. What two types of anger does he identify? Why is there no need to condemn yourself or your wife for experiencing anger?

5. The second step is to admit your anger to each other. Why is it unhelpful to play "Guess My Mood"? Why does your wife deserve to know when she's done something that triggered your anger?

6. The third step is to agree that verbal and physical explosions that attack the other person are inappropriate responses. What do explosive expressions of anger always do? What practical strategy does Dr. Chapman suggest to break the habit of responding explosively to anger? How difficult would it be for you and your spouse to incorporate that strategy into your relationship? Explain.

7. The fourth step in managing anger in a healthy way is to seek an explanation before passing judgment. What examples does Dr. Chapman offer to illustrate the importance of withholding judgment until you hear your wife's side of the story? What personal illustration would you add regarding a knee-jerk reaction or misunderstanding that you regret?

8. The fifth step is to agree to seek a resolution. Think of the last intense disagreement you and your wife had. What kind of direct, loving confrontation would have opened the door to constructive conversation and problem-solving? What would have been an ideal resolution to the conflict?

9. The sixth step is to affirm your love for each other. According to Dr. Chapman, when you and your wife sincerely say "I love you" after anger is resolved, what are you really saying? In situations where a true wrong has been committed, what needs to happen before the anger can go dormant again?

TAKE IT HOME

One of the best ways to limit the destructive power of anger in your life is to understand what tends to make you angry and why. Next to the thermometer below, list some things that commonly stir your anger. Place each one at the appropriate spot on the thermometer to indicate just how "hot" it makes you. At the bottom you might list minor annoyances such as slow drivers in the left lane or Green Bay Packers fans. At the top, you'll list things that make you lose control, which might include being lied to. Next to each item on your list, make a quick note about why it makes you angry.

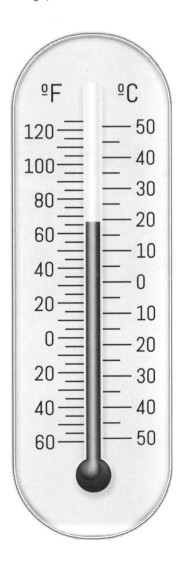

A BETTER IDEA

Here's a list of things you might be tempted to do when you get angry. For each one, come up with a better, more productive idea—one that ultimately benefits your relationship instead of damaging it and brings you closer to your wife instead of driving you apart.

You hold on to your justifiable anger, not saying a word about it, until you can play it like a trump card the next time you and your wife have an argument.

A better idea would be to . . .

You keep ratcheting up the intensity of your anger until your wife gets uncomfortable and surrenders.

A better idea would be to . . .

You refuse to admit that you're angry because you're not in the mood for a confrontation.

A better idea would be to . . .

You walk out of the house without a word of explanation.

A better idea would be to . . .

LOVE CHALLENGE

The best time to discuss anger management with your wife is when neither of you are angry. If the two of you are in a good place this week, how will you broach the topic of dealing with anger in a constructive way? What specific issues will you ask her to discuss? How will you maintain a loving, productive attitude throughout your conversation?

Use this space for more notes, quotes, or lessons learned from the chapter.

OBJECTIVE

In reading this chapter, you will learn how to speak your
wife's primary apology language so that your efforts to say
"I'm sorry" will ultimately strengthen your relationship.

THE ART OF APOLOGIZING

INSTRUCTIONS: Complete this tenth lesson after reading chapter 10 ("The Art of Apologizing," pp. 137–150) of *The 5 Love Languages for Men*.

KEY TERM

Primary apology language: the method of communicating regret and asking forgiveness that most profoundly impacts a person and causes him or her to feel that a relationship has been restored.

OPENING QUESTIONS

1. What's the worst apology you've ever heard? Who offered it, and who was on the receiving end of it? How was the apology received—or rejected? What would have been a better approach?

2. What's something you should have apologized for, but never did? Why didn't you apologize? What do you wish you'd said at the time? Is it too late to say those things now? Explain.

THINK ABOUT IT

3. According to Dr. Chapman, what does a genuine apology have the potential to do—if it's done well? What's the most remarkable result you've ever seen an apology accomplish?

4. The first apology language is expressing regret. What does it mean to express regret? Why is it important for you to feel at least some pain? How can you show your sincerity when you say, "I'm sorry"? What word should never be part of your expression of regret? Explain.

5. The second apology language is accepting responsibility. Why is it so difficult to say, "I was wrong"? What happens when you try to rationalize your behavior? Of the quotes from Jenna, Lizzy, and Mike, which one(s), if any, hit close to home? Explain. Why is it essential to become fluent in the apology language of accepting responsibility?

6. The third apology language is making restitution. According to Dr. Chapman, how is the idea of "making things right" embedded both in our judicial system and in our interpersonal relationships? **"Since the heart of restitution is reassuring your wife that you genuinely love her,"** what is essential for you to do? Give an example of what that might look like in your relationship.

7. The fourth apology language is genuine repentance. What does the word *repentance* mean? What does that mean in the context of an apology in your marriage? How do you speak the language of genuine repentance? What would that sound like in your relationship?

8. The fifth apology language is requesting forgiveness. What are the three reasons Dr. Chapman gives for the importance of requesting forgiveness? On a scale of one to ten, how difficult is it for you to request forgiveness? Explain. How can you get past your discomfort?

9. Dr. Chapman concludes the chapter by writing, **"The art of apologizing is not easy. It doesn't come naturally to most people, but it can be learned by all."** Why does he say **"it's worth the effort"**?

TAKE IT HOME

The apologies people often use after marital conflicts aren't always the best ones available to them. Here are four common apologies you may be tempted to use with your wife. Consider each one carefully and jot down a few thoughts as to why it's not as effective as it could be in healing a rift.

Apology #1:

"My bad."

Apology #2:

"I'm sorry you misunderstood what I was saying."

Apology #3:

"I'm sorry if something I said might have offended you."

Apology #4:

"I'm so sorry. I promise that it will never happen again."

A BETTER APOLOGY

Okay, so you don't want your apology to . . .

- sound too casual, like something you might say to a teammate after missing a wide-open shot;
- suggest that your wife was at fault for mishearing or misunderstanding what you said;
- be too vague or noncommittal, like something written by a lawyer;
- make ridiculous promises that you can't keep.

Now it's time to consider the things you *do* want to say in an apology. Think of a recent argument between you and your wife—or a not-so-recent one that still stands out in your mind.

What was the argument about?

What did you say or do that you regret—or that you want to apologize for? Be specific. Don't just think in terms of what you did, but also consider what your words or actions did to your wife and your relationship.

Put your feelings into words. Write an apology that takes full responsibility for your actions, without trying to make excuses or shift the blame. Acknowledge the hurt you inflicted on your wife and the damage you caused to your relationship. Show an awareness of the things you need to change in yourself so that you don't repeat your mistake. Commit yourself to doing better in the future, but don't make promises you can't keep.

LOVE CHALLENGE

Is there something you need to apologize to your wife for? A thoughtless comment? A betrayal of trust? A benign neglect of some part of your relationship? A blown opportunity to speak her love language? There's no time like the present to put these tips for apologizing to the test. This week, how will you show your wife that you're committed to expressing regret, accepting responsibility, making restitution, showing genuine repentance, and/or asking for forgiveness for hurting her?

Use this space for more notes, quotes, or lessons learned from the chapter.

THE 5 LOVE LANGUAGES FOR MEN LEADER'S GUIDE

CONGRATULATIONS! You're on the cusp of an exciting adventure. You're about to lead a small group through ten studies that will enrich relationships and change lives. And you'll have a front-row seat to it all.

You'll find that every small group presents its own unique challenges and opportunities. But there are some tips that can help you get the most out of any small-group study, whether you're a seasoned veteran or a first-time leader.

1. Communicate.

From the outset, you'll want to give members a sense of how your group dynamic will work. To maximize your time together, group members will need to read each lesson's assigned chapter of *The 5 Love Languages for Men* and then complete the "Opening Questions" (questions 1–2) and "Think About It" section (questions 3–9) *before* the meeting. The "Take It Home" and "Love Challenge" activities should be completed after the meeting.

2. Keep a good pace.

Your first meeting will begin with introductions (if necessary). After that, you'll ask group members to share their responses to the first two "Getting Started" questions. These are icebreakers. Their purpose is merely to introduce the session topic. You'll want to give everyone a chance to share, but you don't want to get sidetracked by overly long discussions here.

The "Think About It" section (questions 3–9) is the heart of the study. This is where most of your discussion should occur. You'll need to establish a good pace, making sure that you give each question its due while allowing enough time to tackle all of them. After you've finished your discussion of the questions, briefly go over the "Take It Home" and "Love Challenge" sections so that group members know what their "homework" will be.

Your next meeting will begin with a brief review of that homework. Ask volunteers to share their responses to the "Take It Home" activities and their experiences in implementing the "Love Challenge." After about five minutes of reviewing your group members' application of the previous lesson, begin your new lesson.

3. Prepare.

Read each chapter, answer the study questions, and work through the take-home material, just like your group members will do. Try to anticipate questions or comments your group members will have. If you have time, think of stories from your own relationship or from the relationships of people you know that apply to the lesson. That way, if you have a lull during your study, you can use the stories to spark conversation.

4. Be open and vulnerable.

Not everyone is comfortable with sharing the details of their relationship with other people. Yet openness and vulnerability are essential in a group setting. That's where you come in. If you have the courage to be vulnerable, to share less-than-flattering details about your own relationship (with your spouse's permission, of course), you may give others the courage to do the same.

5. Emphasize and celebrate the uniqueness of every relationship.

Some group members may feel intimidated by other people's seemingly successful relationships. Others may find that strategies for learning love languages that work for some people don't work for them—and they may get discouraged. You can head off that discouragement by opening up about your own struggles and successes. Help group members see that, beneath the surface, every relationship has its challenges.

6. Create a safe haven where people feel free—and comfortable—to share.

Ask group members to agree to some guidelines before your first meeting. For example, what is said in the group setting stays in the group setting. And every person's voice deserves to be heard. If you find that some group members are quick to give unsolicited advice or criticism when other people share, remind the group that every relationship is unique. What works for one may not work for another. If the problem persists, talk with your advice givers and critics one-on-one. Help them see how their well-intended comments may be having the unintended effect of discouraging others from talking.

7. Follow up.

The questions and activities in this book encourage group members to read through *The 5 Love Languages for Men*, initiate difficult conversations with their spouses, and make significant changes to their relationship routines. You can be the cheerleader your group members need by celebrating their successes and congratulating them for their courage and commitment. Also, by checking in each week with your group members, you create accountability and give them motivation to apply *The 5 Love Languages for Men* principles to their relationships.

THE LOVE SHE CRAVES,
THE CONFIDENCE YOU NEED.

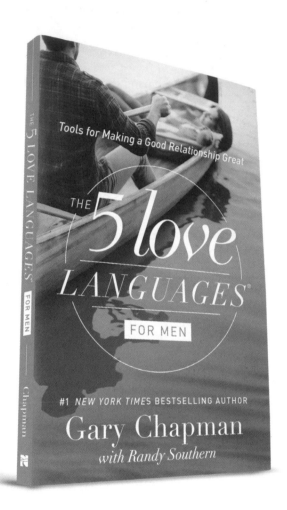